CW01304751

# MY VERY BONES

Nature, Life, Love

Best wishes
Janis

## Poems

by

Janis Martin

ISBN 978-0-244-45203-2

Photography credits:
Front cover - Sally Morningstar
Part One - Janis Martin
Part Two & Back cover - Nigel Ball

Formatted and typeset by Roma Harding

Printed and bound by Lulu.com

This little book is dedicated
to Mother Earth

In offering my reflections in poetic form on Life, Love and Nature, the reader is invited to make a deeply personal connection from the perspective of their own experience. Lack of punctuation is deliberate. The landscape of the Jurassic Coast, where I live in South Dorset, continues to inspire my love of the natural world especially on long walks with my dog Nolly, who brings endless joy in all weathers.

My heartfelt thanks to those who have kindly provided reviews for this little book: Kit Berry, author of the Stonewylde series; Tee Francis, poet and therapeutic writing facilitator; and Danny Nash, publisher of Arkadia magazine (Dorset).

Special appreciation is extended to poet Jay Ramsay, who generously gave his endorsement and good wishes, shortly before his passing.

Janis, January 2019

"Janis Martin's poetry is food for the soul. If you love nature, you will find these poems speak to you so clearly, every word beautifully apt, every sentiment perfectly understood and honoured. I cannot recommend this little book of poetry highly enough – it is magical and speaks directly to your heart. Such a pleasure and delight to read – enjoy!"

– Kit Berry, *author of Stonewylde*

"Janis Martin's stunning debut collection is a spiritual and earthly homecoming. As you listen to her gentle footfall on ancestral byways through 'drifts of woodland filled with the echo of cawing crows', you will hear the sound of a soul in renewal. *My Very Bones* is an intensely personal, poetic journey through the Dorset landscape, in which she embraces the protection of the Green Man and the elements, finding continuity, love and unity in Mother Nature throughout the changing seasons.

"Martin's poetry is an exercise in mindfulness; the reader is invited to rest awhile, breathe deeply and feel the grass beneath their feet. As the poet finds closure and salvation in the natural world, we feel deeply privileged to share in the experience, and bear witness to her joy and rebirth."

– Tee Francis, *Dorset poet*

# MY VERY BONES

## Poems

## Part One

# NATURE

## WHITE SNOW

White snow against the sky
No horizon to be seen
A brilliance so bright
I'm almost blinded
And squint
As a hawk swoops down
And glides to the right
Hovering in the field
The white of his underside
Merging against the sky
Brown feathers
Outline his white body
And I see him clearly
Head hung down
As he scans the field
For any movement
Of something he can eat
I pass him by
As I go past the field
On my way home

## UNDER COVER OF DARKNESS

Moving swiftly
Stumbling
Caught in the brambles
Hidden by darkness
My chest is pained
Breath short
The smell of blood trapped
Echoes of the strike reverberating
Feet pounding
Early morning dew thrust aside
My heart hammering
Clambering and slipping
I leap the lichen clad gate
And onto the dark road ahead
For the briefest of moments
I pause
And turn
To glance at the tenuous slice of light
Creeping through the gloom
And leave the sunrise behind me

## TRANQUILLITY

Butterfly or bird
Way out of reach
I sit and ponder
On what each can see
Flutter or fly
High and low
Enjoying the sunshine
Against the blue sky
I sit and listen
Head to one side
The wondrous sounds
Free and alive
Sheep are bleating
Seagulls call
Bees are humming
A soothing tone
And all the while
Trees rustle and shimmer
Providing a quiet
But deep tranquillity

## THE WITCH TREE

She calls me the Witch Tree
Senses magical spells
And puts her trust in me
Trust in my strength
Supporting lovers leaning in
Offering refuge to the squirrel
Just out of reach
Of the dog below
My fallen leaves
Nourishing the creepy crawlers
Lingering around my roots
Colourful lichen on barren bark
Brings a smile to wandering souls
She puts a trust in me
As my branches reach out to her
At the break of day

## AUTUMN

On a day like today
As the wind begins to blow
Shaking the trees wildly
And crisp golden leaves
Begin to fall softly
Whirling and twirling
To cover the ground
Leaving behind
On their branches
A few lonesome leaves
As Mother Nature lets go
And Autumn arrives

## GRANDMOTHER MOON

Grandmother Moon she winked at me
She made me smile
Dipping and diving between the clouds
Revealing herself in part
A huge silver ball
Brimming with energy
To light up the night
I laughed with delight
Heard her call my name
Inviting me to dance
So filled with glee
I did just that
Never minding the wet grass
Beneath my feet
I kicked off my shoes

And thrilled at the shock
Sensing the freedom
Joy entered my being
As I danced in your light
Placed trust in your wisdom
Beaming with abundance
I whispered to you
Held my hands up high
And felt your gentle smile
Your kiss upon my brow
As a tear of gratitude
Formed in my eye
And in that brief moment
In her lunar embrace
I felt complete

## THE WORLD AWAKENS

In that hour between darkness and dawn
Earth creatures begin to stir
The smallest of mice
Suddenly appears before me
Dashing across my path
He stops abruptly
Then scurries on his way
And with a loud trill
A lively bird launches from a bush
Flying at speed
Skimming the ground
Straight back into cover
Oh, what a surprise greets me next
A rabbit hops across my path
And warily stops to listen
Ears jerking
Whiskers twitching
In a scamper he is gone
Dawn is breaking
The World is awake

## APPEASED SENSES

Clouds
Scud across azure sky
Waves
Lip and lap
Salty spray
Catches on dry lips
Crab claw
Rots in the heat of the day
Fingers
Explore smooth worn pebbles
Lying upon the beach
I smile
Each of my senses appeased

## AS DAY IS ENDING

As day is ending
All is still
I sit atop a barrow
The wind has dropped
No cars rush past
No tractors churn the soil
I slow my breath
I close my eyes
And begin to hear the sounds
Of birds calling out to one to another
Their cries echoing in the woods
Then with a rush of wings
A pheasant bursts through a hedge
Alarmed by a fox
His short sharp barks
Alerting his mate
To a possible feast
Hiding but not hidden
My breath has slowed
My mind is clear
Someone whispers close

Wait, have patience
All is well
And like the Cheshire cat
A huge smile appears before my eyes
My reverie broken
I hear a train rumble past
Far in the distant hills
Through a dip in the valley
Carrying the sound
Back to me
And strange as it may seem
I hear a deep throb
The sonorous beat of drums
I ponder briefly and then smile
As a car passes by
Loud music escaping through its windows
That enters my mind
The voice whispers once more
It's alright, all is well
And now with open eyes
I see the fox

A brown smudge
With both head and tail pointing down
He sniffs and listens
As he picks up a scent
Trailing round the field
A rabbit scurries past
White tail bobbing
Going who knows where?
My breathing steadied
I look around
And wonder where did Time go?
With golden light streaked through with red
The sun has disappeared
And with crisp and silver brightness
The moon rises in the sky
Telling me it's time to go
So slowly I retrace my steps
Through grass now dew covered
And mist falling gently
Knowing that all is well

## BATTLING KINGS

Dark grey skies
Rain steadily falling
Hitting the road
Creating the crowns of battling Kings
As cars pass each other by
Oblivious
To the sights and sounds
That speak to me

## YELLOW CATKINS

Yellow catkins
Weighing heavily in trees
Swaying back and forth
As the cold March wind
Blows through bare branches
Tiny buds
Perched on twiggy ends
Of hazel trees that stand
Shaggy and tatty
Awaiting their first pruning
Looking out at Time
A spring chorus fills the air
A myriad of birds
Singing their hearts out
Competing one against another
I hear pigeons cooing
Bobbing their heads
Chest feathers puffed out
Against the cold

A robin and a blackbird
Both hopping about
Searching for treasures
That wonderful smell
Of freshly cut grass
Makes me breathe deeply
All senses buzzing
With so many impressions
Of all that I feel
Seeing the clusters
Hang proudly
Silhouetted
Against the crisp blue sky
My fingertips freeze
As I stand and watch
Lost in thought
To the world around me
A solitary soul
Never alone

## BLACK BEETLE

Black beetle
Polished armour
Solitary stance

Makes me halt
Makes me smile
Watches out for me

Survivor in a modern world
Teacher, ally down through Time
Evolved through Other Worlds

## THE SPIDER

The rain falls gently as fine mist
Tiny droplets suspended around
A spider's web outside the window
Caught on its delicate threads
In the gentle breeze
The diamond crystal filigree
Becomes alive
As if breathing in and out
But don't be fooled
For in the centre of this net
Is a long-legged solitary spider
Still as still can be
Watching and waiting
With all eight eyes alert
He startles for an instant
As a larger droplet hits his web
And vibrates under the weight
The spider anticipates his prey
Before his senses tell him false alarm
And he settles back to wait

## WINFRITH

The place of my forefathers
A Time stood still

As I glance along the High Street
I see thatched roofs
With Beatle haircuts
Sharp and neatly trimmed

Roses growing upwards
Only tattered petals left
White, with withered edges
As autumn closes in

The road that once was laid as dirt
Now neatly edged with grassy verge
And horses that once clopped along
Replaced by shiny cars

A Time stood still

## TAKING A DEEP BREATH

Taking in a deep breath
Feeling the spring air
Ooze deep into my lungs
Holding it there
Absorbing its Life Force
Eyes closed
Imagining
It fills my body
Then the delight of release
Breathing out
Knowing I will do it all over again
The miracle of Being

## THE HILLTOP

On the hilltop
In the heat of the day
Tall grasses sway
Hiding shy orchids
Among their tall dry stems
Seed heads poised to shed
Their harvest to the wind
Where butterflies flutter
Between the flowers
And settle momentarily
Small tortoiseshell
Adonis blue and marbled white
In summer sunlight
Pass by my eyes
A delight to behold
Walkers on the grassy ridge
A distant mirage up ahead
Shimmer in the haze
Distorted forms that melt away

Swallowed by the far horizon
Long grass and purple thistle
Vetch and yellow rattle
Beckon me to join them
Filling my senses with joy
Vibrations emanating
From the body of the earth
An impulse penetrates and fills me
With a fleeting energy
My mind is full of dreams
My body freed of chains
Painful memories erased
A certain freedom regained
A land consecrated to nature
Sacred stones and ritual ways
Circles of sarsens set in place
Where the land reveals her current
And man connects
To live in harmony

## THE GREEN MAN

A good place to be
Where I know I'll be safe
And come to no harm
I step into the woods
Where all is calm
Tall trees to the left
And more trees to the right
Ferns at my feet
I'm filled with delight
The narrow path bends and twists
It leads me even deeper
Past trickling stream and fallen boughs
Hiding the Woodland Keeper
I see him in his many guises
Animal, sprite and bird
He watches quietly
As I pass this certain tree
Something makes me stop
And listen for his Word
I reach and touch the matted moss
My hand upon the top

I stroke, I rub, and rest my head
My senses explode with joy
For I have found my heart's desire
This Green Man grown now
My head upon his chest
I hear his heart beat loud
He's calling me to join him
Beneath his branches bowed
To make this Man and Wo-man as one
With no shame I sit upon his legs
My love is warm, my love is moist
Against his mossy limb
Moving slowly, moving gently
I feel my passion rise
I know my body loves him
I know my body cries
My head thrown back
My body tenses
I recognize a flashback
And as I tremble with release
I know indeed that we are one

# RAMPARTS

The landscape is like a canvas
Waiting for an artist
To sit and paint and draw
To make a pilgrimage
Collecting treasures along the way
Where memories are kindled
As pathways beckon forth
Urging one to traverse hilltops
Clamber up and over fields
Through drifts of woodland
Filled with the echo of cawing crows
And raucous cries of rooks
Nesting high in tall trees
And overhead a buzzard circling
Revels in flight on rising thermals
Above the hill where cattle graze
The ramparts lined with hoof tracks
Carved deep into the chalky turf
The thin earth tufted with sun-dried grass
Where sheep graze and stare

The seed heads mingle with wild flowers
And vagrant butterflies shimmer
In the onshore breeze
As skylark the sentinel rises
And hovers in the thermals
Remote and tuneful chanting
Heard from afar
A heavenly existence
The hills appear to soften
Blue-green in the summer haze
As distance brings perspective
Before rain clouds begin to gather
Memories of childhood
Play upon one's mind
A once shy child that hid away
Now merges with the ancient hillside
No less mystical and magical
Are the ramparts and barrows
In this time-honoured valley

## SPIRIT RIDER

Right in front of me
Blocking my way
Stands a large black horse
With rider on his back
Sitting tall and silent
A wide brimmed hat
Pulled down low
His black cloak
Flailing high
Leaving two black eyes
Staring straight ahead
Giving no clue as to their owner
His horse rears up
With a snort and squeal
Its misty breath opaque
Swirling in the evening light

It lands back down
And twice stomps his hoof
Brown mane flying
Like snakes in the breeze
The rider sits still firm
Clasping tightly shortened reins
His leather gloves creaking
The beast now quietens
Head held high
I feel no fear and ponder
Why no care nor warning
Before you blocked my path
What Being sent you here?
What message do you bring?
And why a rider dressed in black –
Guardian or foe my friend?

## SEAGULL

Orange eyes
Orange beak
Orange feet
Snow white feathers
Full plump body
Head bobbing
Always on his guard
The slightest morsel
Hits his senses
And down he swoops
The seagull
Screaming in victory

## PEACE

Swirls
Follow curves
Tumbling
Falling
Snaking
Gently
Connecting
Scooping
Around me
Exhilarating
Tingles
Lightly
Calming
Soothing
Reassuring
Offering solace
Tranquillity
Quietly
Moving on

# SALISBURY MILL

Water rushes and gushes
Intent with purpose
As it disappears under the bridge
And there I glimpse
With great delight
A waddling duck
Quacking her babies to order
Their fluffy bodies
Yellow and brown
Cheeping, zooming around
As though on wheels
Curious to every little thing
That catches their eye
Totally oblivious to mother's fear
Of dangers lurking
Plastic bottles, tin cans
Polystyrene debris left on the bank
From homeward boys 'out on the town'
Families picnicking
Without a thought
For Nature

# LIGHTNING

Lightning bolts sear my eyes
Each in quick succession
An energy coursing through me
Alive with power
My body all a-glow
I sense the storm approaching
Distant growls of thunder
Swirling, moving
Sending shivers down my spine
Setting my pulse racing
My warm skin a-tingle
The magnetic energy rises
Pulling me close
As drop by drop the rain falls
Settling on dust and stone
And I smell the damp earth alive

## JUNE EVENING

Evening draws in
The summer air is still
With pinks and golds
Loudly lighting the sky
As I smell the heat of the day
On cooling grass
And the roosting birds
Fill my ears with their lullaby
As I head for home, contented

## LOOK AROUND

Indian summer skies
With hues of blue
And flossy clouds
Forging a picture
Of immense expanse
A tapestry of leaves
Clinging onto trees
Whilst beneath their bowers
Toadstools push through leaf mould
And grasses fade to yellows and browns
Each blade little by little doubling down
September days
Nudging into autumn

## SEPTEMBER

Autumn dipping her toes
Leaves curling, changing colour
Falling to the ground
Swept up in corners
A freshness to the dawn
A sense of peace
Settled and calm
A pause in the seasons
Harvesting thoughts
Time to reflect
Looking forward
Transition
As Nature prepares to sleep

## THE SQUIRREL

Looking from my window
I saw this little chap
Leaping onto fencing
Landing on his toes
Thank goodness
For his great big tail
To balance as he goes
He takes a cautious step or two
Checking what's ahead
Jumping over brambles
Turning back awhile
To stop and feed
Whilst glancing all around
Deciding where to go
Then moving forward
Off he goes
And I'm left wondering
What on earth he seeks?

## HILL FORT

Tilt your head just to one side
And let your eyes go lazy
A whole new world opens-up before you
The silvery lines of cobwebs
Stretching from blade of grass
To blade of grass
Like elfin hurdles
Only visible in the sunshine
The water sprites down by the river
Languishing
Amongst wooden posts and fencing
Watching and waiting
As the water rushes by
Noisily
It divides against the stone pillar
Some of the water escapes
Turning back on itself
Creating ripples in the muddy pond
Around the old gnarled tree
Holding memories from the distant past

Of people passing
Stopping to rest a while
Or lovers sharing time together
Before departing
The Spirit of the tree
Looks down upon them all
Wrapping them in her care
Her autumnal yellowing leaves
Twisting and twirling towards the ground
Gently clacking as they hit the branches
Creating a wonderful blanket beneath
To keep her roots warm until spring
And the ancient burial mound
From times gone by
Sits atop the hill fort
Surrounded
By the safety of the grassy ramparts
The ancestors taking comfort
Their knowledge and wisdom
Contained securely therein

## LEAVES

Brown leaves piled high
Tucked in to a corner
A family of many kinds
Huddled as one
Until a playful gust of wind
Lifts them all into the air
Catching the furls
Tossing and turning
Then slowly landing
I stand and watch
As play unfolds
The wind teasing and taunting
Chasing and catching the leaves
Whisking them all into a whirl
Until the group disperses
When the wind sees me
It's time to move on
To leave the game

## THE OAK TREE

I thought he was just another tree
How very wrong could I be!
Old Man Oak
Is his name
Standing tall
Upright and strong
I lean my brow upon his bark
Feel his wood beneath my hands
As he listens to my thoughts
A truer guide I've yet to find
I will be back, I will return
To share my secrets
With this guardian
Old Man Oak
Green Man
Confidante
Protector

## LOST IN THE WOODS

Sometimes you get lost
Walking alone through the woods
When over ancient barrows
The Ridgeway track distracts
Mind metamorphosis diverts
Your eyes to see images
Of someone else walking in you
Conscious of a transformation
A sense and feeling
Of a former self long gone
An aspect of whose energy remains
Within you of an ancient ancestor
Sharing your journey in the present
Watching progress over unknown paths
Guiding you to find your way back

## NOVEMBER

Far from the madding crowd
An unexpected autumnal glow
Warms my face
As birds sing with delight
Enjoying the respite
From relentless rain
Driven by the harsh north wind
Crows caw
Traffic roars
A gust of wind blows my hair
Covering my face
Hiding my eyes
I hear the rustle of bulrushes
The crack of a branch
A dog leaping as he barks
My hair parts enough to see
Him land in green slime
Frantic paddling across the pond
Blue ball clenched between his teeth
He thinks I want to play
And then he's gone

## WINTER SOLSTICE

Standing in the silence
Breathing in the still
Two friends reflect
As Solstice night draws in
The fog lightly hangs
Casting a silvery hue
Sheep quietly bleating
An owl lets out a screech
Echoing in the wooded canopy
Darkly silhouetted against the night sky
No stars, no moon this night
All is hushed

## ON THE HORIZON

As the sun begins to rise
A swathe of golden light
Seeps into the velvet purple
Of the breaking dawn
A silvery crescent moon hangs
Guarded by four sentinel stars
Sparkling, shimmering, shining proudly
I stand quite still
Then raise my arms
And with barely a whisper
I give my thanks
For the blessing of being alive
The air is still
Holding its breath
Only the chirrup of early risers
Breaks the silence with their song
Excited to greet a brand-new day
Overhead I hear the wing beat
Of a flight of birds
Against the stillness of the morning sky
And know the day has begun

## DECEPTION

I started the day
With an aim in mind
I was to walk a long way
Twenty miles my goal

The afternoon that greeted me
Looked perfect for this plan
A blue sky beckoned, wispy clouds
Drawn along by gentle breeze

But stepping outside the door
The realisation hit me in an instant
The heat from the sun was sweltering
An arid dryness in my mouth told me
It was going to be a tough walk

## A MOMENT IN TIME

A moment in Time
A small girl skips this way
Her flowery dress
Billowing as each step falls
Pressing lightly into a patch of grass
Oblivious to the river by her side
Rippling and twinkling in the sun
Diamonds and crystals
Caught up for a single moment
Rushing past to an unknown destiny
Stopping and bending forward
Locked in a world of her own
Picking at white daises
With precise intent
She plucks each petal
One by one
Tossing them skywards
Then watches
As caught up in a breeze
They twist and twirl
Before gently landing back to earth

## MOTHER EARTH

If I laid upon the grass
If I let my heart beat close
If I closed my eyes so tight
And spread my arms about
Would She tenderly hold me?

If I laid upon the grass
If I cleared my thoughts
If I slowed my breath right down
And paused and really listened
Would She softly hear me?

If I laid upon the grass
If I whispered words of love
If I touched my lips to the ground
And kissed softly Mother Earth
Would She gently embrace me?

If I laid upon the grass
If I tried to pull her to me
If I held her tightly close
And never let her go
Would She forever hold me?

# THE CREATOR

An artist must have passed that day
Armed with a palette of heavenly colours
Reds and oranges, yellows and golds
Daubed by his thumb onto the green hills
Overlaid on autumnal hues
A blue so deep and brilliant
Reflected in the clear water
Of a stream that twists and turns
Lost in a world of its own
Bubbling calmly along the valley
Diamond droplets bouncing in the sun
Behind a bend I see the sky
And then so nearly missed
Two eagles swooping into view
One behind the other

Gliding along the river bank
Majestic finger-tipped wings
Stretched far out wide
With white heads tipping forward
I see the contrast of yellow beaks
Against the iridescent black feathers
Of contoured powerful bodies
Such beauty in their perfect form
So elegant and streamlined
With feet tucked close into their chests
These birds of prey take flight
And disappear from view
Leaving me breathless and in awe
My heart beating with wonder
At the creation of Mother Nature

## ALONG THE RIDGEWAY

Along the Ridgeway track
She strides out on flinty pathways
Past barrows of the ancient dead
Up hill, down dale
Past hedgerows crowned with thorns
And fields of golden corn
With random poppies strewn
Wild flowers thrusting scent
Into the summer air
The butterflies and birds
Perched in leafy bower and branches
Watch her pass quietly unnoticed
The curious deer look on
And a startled badger
Scuttles back into the undergrowth
Whilst on a post an owl is poised
Curiosity aroused
Then flies away to seek his prey
She stops to quench her thirst
And lays upon the ground
To feel the soft vibrations

Absorb the energy of earth
A journey of discovery
Searching to find herself
This pilgrimage a secret quest
To link herself with destiny
Her past and future lives explored
Looking back to where she's been
Forward to the great unknown
A touch of fear within her
A quiet confidence in freedom
Newly found she walks with care
To far horizons, pastures fresh
And meadows lush with green
Within a copse of ancient trees
A silent Spirit friend beside her
Always there to help navigate
And guide her through the maelstrom
To calm her troubled Soul
Bringing peace and comfort
To her weary mind and bones

## ARTHUR'S STONE

Long since gone
Spirits linger
Still at home
Message given
Sorted out
Listen closely
To the stones
They do not shout
Gifts abound
Out of sight
Pay attention
Seek them out
Safe haven
Rebirthed
Arthur's Stone
Takes flight

## A GLIMPSE OF THE PAST

I close my eyes
The sun burns through
And scarlet clouds my vision
I try to imagine who I am
Is a past life living in me?
I have to wonder
At a brief glimpse
A strange feeling
Of magic in the air
A mystery
That feels so real
A history I can't explain

# WALKING

White fibres on her black poncho
Catch in the brambles as she passes
The tiny thorns hold fast
As if protecting the last remaining berries
She keeps on walking
Tugging free, snagging the wool
Enjoying the freedom of her journey
Thinking twice before plucking a fruit
Tainted by the fumes of speeding cars

Drinking in the beauty around her
Teasels brown with colour faded
Grouped tightly proud and tall
Red haws on spindly fingers
Daring to invade their space
Senses alert she lifts her head
And breathes in the sweet sickly fragrance
Tree hugging ivy in flower
With clusters of light green orbs

She keeps on walking
A smile erupts as she espies a rabbit
Glancing around nose twitching
He hops cautiously into a garden
Hoping he might find feast galore
Amongst the reddened and yellowing leaves
Of a cherry tree standing firm
Adorned with red vine tinsels
Its trunk gowned in green

Turning the corner down the hill
She crosses a murky river
The water yellow-green and stagnant
Something has blocked its flow
A butterfly basks on a wall
In the last heat of the autumnal sun
Three great turkey oaks come into view
Serving as sentinels, guarding the wood
The ground beneath littered with fallen leaves

Scuffing her feet with childish delight
She kicks through the drifts with wild abandon
Neither thinking nor caring if she is seen
Finding great joy in this moment
She carries on walking
Her heart lifts when just along the path
An Old Friend comes into view
But someone has pinned a notice
Pricking its trunk with pins

She whispers 'I'm sorry'
And wraps her arms around his trunk
Gently stroking his bark
'I'll come again another day'
Nearly home, nature offers one last gift
Toadstools by the dozen
Taking the place of two old trees
Long since gone
Letting her know that life goes on

## MIST

Floating above the fields
A delicate mist descends
Like a kiss
Lazily tracing natural curves
Leaving speckled dew
Calming
Cleansing
Winter morning fog
Gently chills my brain
As trees loom up
Through the haze
As if from nowhere
And beyond
A veil of nothingness
From heaven

## EARLY MORNING

Darkness gives way to early dawn
Sunlight glistens
Light plays through the crystal
Of early morning dew
Suspended
On a single blade of grass
Reflecting like a mirror
Before it slides
Dropping in an instant
Onto my bare feet

## WINTER'S NIGHT

A wonderful clear winter's night
Here I am, feeling the breeze
Cooler on my face than before
Crystal stars adorning the dark sky
Hanging on a shimmering veil
The tiniest sliver of silvery moon
Teasing, taunting, hinting
Everything is as it should be
And only just arriving
This new moon
Heralds the coming season

## AS NIGHT DRAWS IN

As night draws in
The sun goes down
Dropping behind the Ridge
A golden ball of fire no more
As the last of the day's heat
Sinks into the ground
Driving the midges
In throbbing swarms
All around me
Bird song echoes
In the valley
Bouncing off hills
Calling their final tune
Ready to settle
Safely hidden
Protected by thicket of hedge
Sitting silently
Deep in thought
I watch and wait
My patience rewarded

As two eyes
Peer cautiously
Nose twitching
A female deer
Walks timidly
Into the open
Standing still
Silently listening
Head tilted
Eyes blinking
Suddenly
A car rushes past
A few metres away
With a leap and a bound
All too quickly
She is gone
Her image remains
Forever clear
A gift

## TREES TALK

They say that trees might talk to us
And I believe they do
But not in words or sentences
Neither muttered nor out loud
Just stop and listen to their sound
The air is filled with music
The trees alive are all around
Their leaves on top
Chased by wind
Sound like cymbals
Kissed by bristle brush
I hear old branches creak and groan
With deep and wooden timbre
As broken branches
From times gone by

Lie firmly wedged
Like two old gentlemen
I hear the neighbours croon
Without a pause in perfect unison
The birds fulfil the chorus role
Bursting forth with lusty song
With chirrup, whistle, tweet or trill
They fill the woods around me
With a thousand songs of joy
When I go out walking in the woods
Surrounded by the verdant trees
I pause to take a breath and wait
To hear the magic of the symphony
Playing from within

## THE ARTIST

He sits
Intent
Intensely
Scanning the scene
With concentrated focus
Setting it to canvas
Together with his magic box
Of brushes, pencils, pens
Busily sketching
Recording the moment
Before painting in colour
Blue hues and green
Brown, white and cream
Lost to this world
Found in his element

# LOST IN THOUGHT

The rush of water alerts me
Whilst walking through the field
Alive with vibrant colours
Daises competing with dandelions
Pink clover swaying in the still warm breeze
And there a low bridge
Spans the meandering stream
Twinkling with magical rainbows
Caught at day's end
As the sun begins its slow descent
Tall trees holding back the sandy banks
Woody tendrils dip their toes in the water
Burying themselves in the muddy bed
Resting my arms upon the cast iron rail
For the briefest of moments
Lost in thought
I wonder if others have done the same?
Imagining those who will take the time
From their busy lives to pause
And give thanks to Mother Nature
As she goes about her business

## NATIONAL POETRY DAY

The clouds hang heavily above the clifftop
Thick and dark, almost foreboding
Yet mirroring along their length
Colours and shapes of pure delight

I hold no fear of storms or thunder
Of wild and angry skies
For me, a beauteous gift
From the generous Gods on High

The wind has dropped, the leaves fall still
Some rooks are perched in treetops
They watch, they wait, their eyes a-blink
Silence all around

That first fat drop falls on my foot
And splays with glistening force
A tiny lake of minute form
Trickles to the earth

I tilt my head and breathe in deep
I smell the damp and dusty air
The drops fall faster, faster, faster
But not as fast or wild as me

I run, I jump, I spin around
The rain soaks through my hair
It drips right through and down my face
I'm overcome with glee

## THE RAIN

Sometimes it's good to feel
The rain upon your face
The wind through your hair
And blood flow through your veins
As fingers wipe away the raindrops
Falling from your nose
Running down your face
As it soaks your skin and hair
Merging with sweat and toil
All feels damp and warm
Feet keep walking forward
Vision blurs as eyes fill with tears
And see the world
In a different light
Of soft contours and smooth edges
A kaleidoscope of rainbow-colours
As white light shatters
Into seemingly shapeless crystals
Of beauty and form

## THE WORLD ON MY THUMB

'To see a World in a grain of sand
And Heaven in a wild flower'
Said William Blake
A whole world could fit on my thumb
I got to thinking
The tiniest of planets
Brimming with Life
As creatures hustle and bustle
Going about their day
Oblivious to my watchful eye
I could peer with intent
Head to one side
Eyes screwed tightly
Trying to steal a glance
Of new vistas yet to be explored
But who am I to interfere
To add my two pennies' worth
To a World so tiny yet infinite
That there'd still be room for me?
Yes, I like that idea!

## THE LAKE

Gentle whispers of the water
Drawing my attention close
To ripples from the furthest shore
Landing at my feet
The breeze singing her song
As leaves rustle high and low
Dappling the silvery light
Most blessed Lady
Shapeshifter
Enchantress
I hear your voice
I hear your call

## ROCK POOL

Brimming with life
A perfect world
Breezes tease
A shimmering strand
Of abandoned seaweed
Swaying in ripples
Casting shadows
A solitary creature
Shelters
Barely visible
The limpet
Waits for the tide
To return its freedom
And find new home

## A MERMAID

I perch upon the sharp edge of a rock
Uncomfortable but alert
To the crystal-clear waves
Washing upon the sand
In constant involuntary motion
Teasing the fronds of seaweed
Rippling back and forth
Like flags along the sea bed
A silence all about me
Just the soft lapping of the sea
The heat from the sun
Warming my legs
Creating a hot spot
Yet my back is cold
No birds, no people
Alone on this beach
All is quiet to my searching eyes
Just a gentle breeze
Blowing in from the harbour
Pushing the waves along the shore

I hear the tinkle of a bell
Sounding its warning on a fishing boat
As tiny flies, barely visible
Silent to my ear, hover in the air
Wings furiously beating
Whilst surrounded by pebbles
Brown, yellow, black, white, grey, pink
Round ones, flat ones
Some pitted and jagged
Others smooth and worn
By the waves washing up the sand
And the sun catches the sparkle
Of occasional crystal or sea glass
And the smallest of shells
Some whole, some broken
A myriad of treasures
Scattered in between the pebbles
Draped with blackened weed
Await the soft caress of a wave
And I think of being a Mermaid

## WEST BAY

Heels sink deep into the orange gravel sand
The rolling crunch of boots against stone
Each footprint leaving tiny pools
Only to be dissolved by the next wave
Crashing headlong up the beach
Dogs running, barking, bounding
Challenging the water as it rushes back
Washing over colour-charged stones
Transforming each into shiny treasures
Zillions of air bubbles creating gentle foam
As waves smash against pebbles in the depths
Then with a quiet 'pop pop popping'
Disappear for the briefest of time
And repeat again with the thunderous crash
Of the next wave coming into shore

## A JOURNEY

The start of a journey
At the brink of a mountain peak
Just a flurry of snow atop
The air almost painfully clear
There stands a woman
Who with a smile
Reaches out her hand
To a small girl
Who tightly clasps
The grown-up fingers
In innocence and complete trust
Looking into the woman's eyes
She sees a protector
Someone who will love and guide her
As the two start their descent
Hand in hand, one step at a time
Down the spiralling pathway
Of smooth red earth
No rocks or stones to trip them up
Walking with purpose
To an unknown destination

## THE GRAND CANYON

With frustrating sadness
I'm stuck in this city of noise
Of bright lights
And crowds of people
Traffic fumes
Discarded litter
Like a prisoner
Trapped here in Las Vegas
The sight of distant mountains
Teasing me
With unknown freedom
Two more days
I have to wait
Holding onto a patience
I don't believe in
And soon enough
Excitement mounts

I step from the bus
My feet firmly planted
On the rocky edge
Inhaling deeply
Eyes closed tight
I briefly pause
Savouring that moment
Before eagerly
Scanning the valley
The vista before me
Alive with a thousand hues
Of greens and browns
Yellows and golds
Befitting the majesty
Of the Grand Canyon

## AS OLD AS…

As old as the rocks
As old as the cracks
As old as the cliffs
As old as the stacks
As old as the sea
As new as each wave
As it hits the shore
As it speaks to me

## QANTUTA

Qantuta is quite exotic
The national flower of Peru
Evoking passion and beguile
Her bell-shaped flowers hang
Enticingly complete with skirt
That flips up around the edges
Her bloom inviting closer view
The oranges, pinks and yellows
Reflect the rise and setting sun
Strength and depth of colour
The sacred flower of the Inca
Filled with warmth and light
Each a basic need of man
Qantuta unites as One

## Part Two

# LIFE – LOVE

## ANTICIPATION

Flip flop, flip flop
Sandals flopping down the road
Arms swinging, hips swaying
She lifts her head, flings back her hair
Words and images flood her mind
In anticipation of what's to come
Then she sees his figure on the bench
Sat there, looking about
She stands a moment, taking in the scene
Excitement builds, her body a-tremble
In anticipation of what's to come
Her pulse quickens, her heart races
She closes her eyes, holds her breath
Clasping her hands to her chest
Then she slowly
Purposefully opens her eyes
Parts her lips
To great joy!
As he smiles his welcome
In anticipation of what's to come

## TICKING CLOCK

In the still of night
The clock ticks a comforting tock
All is quiet
Nothing stirs
I lay back and listen
Straining for the slightest sound
The pictures of the day
Playing through my mind
Putting events in order
The computer screen
The tap of the mouse
A rustle of papers
Laughter in the background
Somebody making a joke

My walk at lunchtime
Drinking in the sights as I pass
One foot in front of the other
A well-trodden path
People in the supermarket
The beep of the tills
The hustle and bustle
Of paying and packing
Some smiling, others frowning
Struggling with bags, kids and all
Every face telling a story
Then back to the computer
'Tap tap tap' at the end of the day
As the clock ticks a comforting tock

# THE MAN

She walks along her chosen path
Following a track
Guided between hedgerows
Fragrant flower blossom filling the air
All answering a call within her soul
And so she wanders further
The rolling hills holding her
In their peaceful valley
The gentle breeze caressing her
Leading her through a wooden gate
To walk barefooted in a meadow
The wind blowing softly through the grass
Disturbing butterflies
That flutter about her head
Touching her for a brief encounter
With painted wings
Before flying away into open skies
Then for just a moment, she pauses
Rests her body upon the ground
To feel the energy of Earth's warm bed

Whilst overhead a raven watching
With keen eye and faithful heart
Her guardian never out of sight
She stirs, looks back along a lane
To see the golden glow of evening light
Above a distant city
The setting sun catching the glint
Of stone on gleaming towers
Yet no memories exist
Of her being there before
And so she walks into a future
Until now unseen
Skywards the raven attends her every step
Gliding, calling, reassuring
For on the horizon stands a figure
No turning back, not now
She has far to go
A sense of calm descends
And stepping forward
She walks to meet the waiting man

## TODAY

Waves lapping
Not quite crashing
Cars rushing
Motorbike back-firing
Children giggling
Squealing, screaming
Oars splashing
Helicopter droning
Dads instructing
Mums chatting
Crisp packet rustling
Fizzy drink popping
Something beeping
And all the while
The sun blazing down
As I sit on the rocks
In total silence

## THE OFFICE

The whir of the printer
The whir of the printer
Disturbing a silence
A break in the chatter
The clatter of keys on a keyboard
The snap of the jaw of a closing stapler
The ringing of phones
The slamming of doors
The clink of a spoon
The rustle of papers
Being shifted and sifted
Pushed into envelopes
Dropped into bins
The whir of the printer
Always present
An irritating clatter
A constant familiar friend
Churning out words
All those words
The whir of a printer
The whir of a printer

## A DRAUGHT

I feel a draught
Coming through the window
Slyly teasing its way in
Around my ankles
Across my back
And without a conscious thought
The hairs on my arms begin to rise
Making a stance against the chill
I rub my limbs with intent and purpose
And the body hairs relax
Falling flat and snug against my skin
Now isn't that a thing?

# OVER A PINT

A thousand conversations
Of granny and granddad
Shared memories
Of holidays past
Youngsters with tattooed arms
Petting and loving
Shrill laughter
Stark and loud at a shared joke
And a Collie gets excited
A new puppy to be admired
The view changes as I turn my head
The Channel with its myriad of hues
Blues, greens and silver
Contrast gracefully against the backdrop
Of huge, commanding cliffs
Falling stones, open quarries
Grass scattered in between
Glasses of golden cider
Held firmly in hand
As Portland drinks
To warmth from the glorious sun

## THE BALLET DANCER

She stands quite still
Glancing around
The five-year old at dancing class
Her legs are thin
In thick pink tights
Pumps tied neatly round her ankles
The music starts
She swings her arms
Eager to get started
The movement grows
Excitement in the air
When teacher asks for silence
The children form a circle
Clammy hand in clammy hand
On tippy toes
Intent upon their faces
The little girl looks all around
Seeking out her granddad

Certain that he sees her
Her face lights up
A great big beam
Revealing tiny teeth
With arms out straight
They plonk their feet
Too young yet for fine placing
The teacher claps
To mark out time
And toes point stumbling forward
The smiles soon fade
Replaced by thought
As each child gains her balance
And granddad watches with delight
His face displays such joy
At this little girl
His little girl
His eyes begin to moisten

## CLEAR NIGHT SKY

A wide-open darkness
Bursting with pulsating stars
The light spilling over
Falling into my eyes
Looking deeply
Intently
Focusing
Clear night sky
Penetrating your soul
My love rushing
Connecting
Never letting go

## HOLD TIGHT

At the end of the journey
I felt an ache
Life had ended for a while
Taken a dip
But inevitably
It will take another turn
Memories flood in
The cliché of laughter
Of tears and joy
Ripped apart by grief
In all its guises
Holding tight
Staying firm
Until a glimmer of light
Breaks gently
Through the darkness
And sorrow begins to fade

## SATURDAY GIRL

Saturday morning
My dad touched me
He laid his head in my lap
Moved his hand under my skirt
Sneakily, quietly
To the tops of my legs
My dad touched me
For the first time
Over forty years ago

Another Saturday
My dad touched me
Bumping along the white, chalky lane
He stopped the minibus
He said I could drive
But I had to sit between his legs
While mum was back at work
My dad touched me
Over forty years ago

I got myself a Saturday job

## BELIEVE IN ME

Void, cancelled, simply annulled
An empty space
Just passing through time
Alone is not a bad way to be
To come close to sharing oneself
Never completely revealing the whole
A translucent veil worn
By a heart-torn soul
Controlled by another
Crossing my path
At a moment in time
Becoming a presence in my life
Now questions must wait
As time stands still
In my mind I must trust
The wisdom and mystery
The voice able to reason
And forever believe in Me

## BUBBLES

Each bubble is different
Each bubble the same
They all hold a rainbow
They all hold a dream
A froth of collective bubbles
Separate yet as one
Should a bubble break away
And head for the skies
From what is it escaping?
Following a path
It doesn't really matter
Each journey is unique
And if that bubble bursts
I won't be sad or sorry
Since as it falls
Downwards to the Earth
Its dream is shared with all

## DECISIONS

Happy or sad
Burdened but glad
Decisions
Taking months
Sometimes days
At best hours to reach
Decisions
Headache
Heartache
Weary bone ache
Decisions
Sleepless nights
Restless days
Decisions
Tangled
Knotty
Or in plain sight
Life always brings
Decisions

## TIME

There's a feeling in the air
A sense of something
Not quite there
I can't sit still
I stir and fidget
My mind churning
A million thoughts
Each fighting for space
Feeling Time is speeding up
Racing recklessly forwards
Jumping over walls and fences
Barriers keeping Mankind here
People all around me
Talking, chortling
Laughing loudly
Sharing experiences
And having fun

But my place isn't there
As I sense another's call
Unspoken words
Are yet but a whisper
I have to take a pause
And figure out a meaning
Beyond the chaos
Surrounding
An uncertain outlook
The promise
Of a conjoined life
I feel the pull
And just beyond my grasp
I see a path clearly
As if for the first time
Meandering in the distance
Leading me on a journey

## SLEEP TIME

In the early hours
It's dark in my room
Night has drawn in
The curtains are closed
I hear the wind gust
And howl down the chimney
Rattling the door latch
Coming over in waves
Leaving in silence
My eyes are shut tightly
There's only my breathing
Until something alerts me
Making me stir
I turn my head
And take a wary glance
There's a glimmer at the window
A twinkle of light
The streetlight winking
Inviting me over
Tempting me to move

I push back the covers
And stretch out my legs
Tiptoeing softly across the room
Floor boards are creaking
Saying 'you're not alone'
The single beam beckons
Fingers of light
Exploring the backdrop
Against this dark night
Now all is quiet, the air is still
No wind and no rain
No people are out there
At this early hour
If I left this room
Who would know
I'm not always a prisoner
And go on adventures
Breaking the rule that declares
Night time should be
Sleep time

## IN THE FIELDS

I give you love from the fields
The corn crushed against my back
Grandfather Sun, firmly held
In the expanse of blue sky
He sends down flares of golden heat
Whilst surrounding hills envelop us
Protect us, shelter us
Emerald green against vast skies
Glancing over your shoulder
I see an immense shadow
A bird of prey suspended
Looking down just to check
We are but of little consequence
His prey hiding elsewhere
Unaware its time is up

## FIRE

Orange motion
Yellow-green
Ripples of heat
Flickering flames
Rushing up
Trembling down
Sparks leap
Blue and white
Hissing
Snaking
Blistering crackle
Hypnotic sway
Holding tightly
Binds my thoughts
Safely locked down

## LIFE

I'm here at a standstill
Perceiving the stranger that is myself
Having reached the end of a beginning
Experiencing memories from the future
Expansive thoughts that empty my brain
Like waking to the death of birth
Heat from the cold, hunger from food
All in stark monochrome reversal
As millions of people shout out in silence
It becomes worryingly easy
To answer the question
What is Life?

## THE SMELL OF SILENCE

Blaring silence
Ear-popping quietness
I crane my head
Strain my ears
To hear the silence
A calm that blinds me
Makes goose pimples rise
Upon my arms
And steals my voice
Yet I can smell it
The odour of silence
Enshrouded by barren air
A dull hush
Emits all around me
From the maelstrom of life
As I smell the silence

## FEELING SMALL

Sometimes
I feel quite small
Most humbled
By the challenges
Faced in the World
As people survive
Such disasters
And famines
I stand in awe
At the wonders of Life
The intricacies of living
The simplicity of being
To believe in hope
In a higher power
We see goodness
Such kindness
Amidst the horrors
Of bloody wars
And turmoil
And fear

Others survive
Illness and pain
Bereavement
The loss of a child
Or a loved one
Some part of a life
Destroyed by Man
People survive
And then there's me
Just me
One of billions
Like ants
All connected
One to another
Those who are left
We are the people
Who survive
All going on around us
And worry and fret
About such small things

## MY POPPY

Scarlet petals soft and smooth
Reaching upwards
From a deep, dark centre
So deep, so dark
Glistening with moisture
Caught in the early morning dew
My poppy, pink and mauve
Reaches out
From a deep, dark centre
So deep, so dark
She glistens with moisture
Caught on the joyous pleasure of union

## MY SOUL

Today I find my soul
In the best place ever
The best place it can be
Tomorrow may be different
But today is all I see
To start each day afresh
Seeking new challenges for my Soul
Sustaining self as I learn and grow
Life's lessons may be painful
Sometimes filled with joy
Yet how could I ever reach this place
Without nourishing where I came from
And knowing what I know?

## MY PRINCE

He wears no suit of armour
He rides no handsome steed
He carries no flowing banner
He has no shield of gold

My Prince, he lives in joyful hearts
He rides our wildest dreams
Carrying our deepest love
He protects our yearning souls

## MY MAN

Kind

Funny

Playful

Gifted

Creative

Supportive

Compassionate

Understanding

Considerate

Thoughtful

Generous

Youthful

Exciting

Inspiring

Tender

Caring

Loving

Gentle

Warm

Man

## MY LITTLE ONE

He said you had to leave me
He said you could not stay
But really, truly, honestly
I dreaded that awful day...

You weren't supposed to be here
He didn't want you around
But, oh my precious little one
If only you could have made some sound...

They said you had to leave me
And quite a lot I cried
Because, my special little one
You know how hard I tried...

It will pass, they told me
It is all for the best
I could not move past the heartache
The pain inside my chest...

Those days were just surreal
So little time to say goodbye
Happiness turned to sorrow
My life a hazy blur, not to question why...

Although I had to move on
A forward step each day
I will always remember you, little one
But you'll soon forget, they say...

## THE SLEEPING CHILD

All is quiet
This dead of night
The child besides me sleeps
The only sound is gentle breath
A sigh escapes her lips
She dreams a dream
Of great adventure
Flinging out an arm
Kicking out her feet
I can only smile in wonder
With eyes tightly closed
As tears run down my cheeks
The ghost of the child
My little girl
Her memory
Forever lingers

## LOVE

I hold you in my heart
Beating out our song
My arms embrace your soul
Our love is one on one
A light surrounds our lives
Across the empty miles
I yearn to fill the gap
And hold you close again
Only then I'd feel it's safe
To dream of you this night

## ACROSS THE OCEAN

Miles across the ocean
Miles across the sea
Miles stretch out forever
I know you're there for me
Happy but I'm also sad
As I know it is for you
This very special family time
Their visits very few
Yet my heart is laden heavy
Feeling so alone
A tender reminder
Of how my love has grown
It will not be forever
I know this to be true
And when next we meet
I'll no longer be feeling blue

## I AM WITH YOU

I am awake
Are you asleep?
To where do you go in your dreams?
Perhaps you're a prince
So gallant and fair
Seeking a truth
To share with the world?
Maybe a magician or wizard
Casting a spell
To enchant a princess or maid?
Has a femme fatale
Captured your heart?
A fairy tale
Of castles and steeds
Or an earthly tale
Of woodlands and rivers?
Wherever you go
Know this to be true
Until your dreams fade
I'm always with you

## LOVE IS

I feel this sense
Of no control
My heart connected
My mind distorted
My soul is ever yours
A love that cares
Supports and nurtures
Endlessly gives
With utter desire
For your happiness
Mine too
I remind myself
Fulfilment for us both
My trust is sure
My heart is pure
My love is unconditional

## A DULL ACHE

The dull ache
The heavy heart
A quiet sadness
Behind my eyes
My world has paused
My light has dimmed
I wish I could tell you
What's important to me
Right here, right now
Because
It happens to be You

## LOOK UP

Look up
With sadness
Look up
With worry
Look up
With doubt
Look up
Feeling scared
Look up
Look up
See brightness
Look up
See lightness
Look up
A perfect sky
Look up
With a smile
Beguile
Look up

## IT'S OVER

It's time to give up on you
On our love now turned to dust
Our life together such a lie
This is my time to say goodbye
Days together, days apart
Days that hold a broken heart
So many shattered dreams
Stored carefully out of sight
Covered over so as not to cry
In sadness as darkness descends
Recalling memories one by one
Each moment of light turning to a sigh
Next comes all the times we kissed
Now placed alongside a forgotten list
Of times I looked at you and asked
All those questions on my mind
Why could I not read the signs?
Those deep brown eyes so full of deceit
I gave you all I had and tried to make it work
Now I know that all that's left
Are memories from a distant past

## SADNESS

Now here's a thing
Don't you know
That life has changed
Hidden from sight
Whilst all the while
I know I'm right
Aware of issues
Time is a healer
Endless patience
Staying focused
Staying calm
Avoid the fight
Each day
A living battle
An anxious nightmare
Without a base
A place
To call my own

More lonely
Than ever imagined
Surrounded by friends
Loved ones
Offers of help
Support
And kindness
People willing
To hold my hand
But this is my journey
I must travel alone
Many a mountain
To climb
Feeling my way
As a new dawn awaits
To brighten the day
I am ready to face
Whatever comes next...

## CHAKRAS

As I close my eyes
A myriad of colour enters my Body
A vibrant rainbow of my very own
The gentle warmth of energy
Comes over me in ripples and waves
A blaze of whiteness surrounds my crown
Its brilliance lifts my Soul
The soft hue of purple velvet cloth
Encircled by a halo
Sits behind my brow
Bringing vision to my third eye
A forgiving and tender blue
Offers clarity to my voice
The Love of emerald green
Vibrates in unison with the rhythm
Of my beating Heart
And feeds my understanding

A yellow sunburst
Floods my solar plexus
Releasing anxiety and fear
Followed by an orange sacral glow
Igniting my creativity with fire
And finally, a deep redness
Settles into the very base of my Being
Bringing passion and grounding
Flowing through my feet
Connecting me to Mother Earth
A rainbow of chakra colours
Protecting and guiding
Supporting, nurturing
Teaching and healing
My Spirit, my Soul
My All
With Love

## MY STORY WEAVES

I am of this world
My story weaves
My connection reinforced
As life enfolds my being
I sweep my arms
And grasp
Just out of reach
An embrace
Of entwining limbs
I sense the essence
The softness
Of the feminine
Encapsulated in warmth
Released and overwhelmed
Growth and energy
Caged by protection
Sheltered in its expanse
Leaving my soul free

## HOW DO I LOVE THEE?

'How do I love thee?'
Asked Elizabeth Barrett Browning
'Let me count the ways
I love thee to the depth and breadth and height
My soul can reach...'
Her words so eloquent
A romantic gentle-hearted flow
My own words plain
And direct by comparison
Reflective yet more to the point
How do I love thee?
With my Body
With my Mind
And my Soul
That makes three ways –
A Trinity for thee

## REVIEWS

**Kit Berry** – author of Stonewylde series of five novels https://stonewylde.com/

**Tee Francis** – poet and therapeutic writing facilitator https://feelwrite.co.uk/

**Danny Nash** – independent magazine publisher (Dorset) www.arkadiamags.co.uk

**Jay Ramsay** – poet, writer, tutor and psychotherapist (1958-2018) www.jayramsay.co.uk

## PHOTOGRAPHY

**Sally Morningstar** – www.stardustphotography.uk

**Nigel Ball** – https://www.nigelaball.com

To contact **Janis Martin**

Facebook: Janis Martin - Poet
Email: janismartin.poet@outlook.com

*DID2503253*

L - #0078 - 260419 - C0 - 175/108/7 - PB - DID2503253